LIFE WITH A WID⬤WER

LIFE WITH A
WIDWER

OVERCOMING UNIQUE CHALLENGES AND
CREATING A FULFILLING RELATIONSHIP

ABEL KEOGH

BEN LOMOND
PRESS

Published by
Ben Lomond Press
Copyright © 2013 by Abel Keogh
All rights reserved

Cover design by Francine Eden Platt of Eden Graphics, Inc.
Cover design Copyright © 2013 by Abel Keogh

Opinions expressed in this book are those of the author.
ISBN 10: 0615779050
ISBN 13: 978-0615779058

BOOKS BY ABEL KEOGH

RELATIONSHIP GUIDES

Dating a Widower: Starting a Relationship with a Man Who's Starting Over

Marrying a Widower: What you Need to Know Before Tying the Knot

Life with a Widower: Overcoming Unique Challenges and Creating a Fulfilling Relationship

NOVELS

The Third

MEMOIR

Room for Two

TABLE OF CONTENTS

INTRODUCTION

I'VE ANSWERED THOUSANDS OF EMAILS from women who are in relationships with widowers. Despite the different backgrounds and circumstances of those who email me, many of the same problems arise over and over. Whether it's the widower updating the late wife's Facebook page or the memorial tattoo declaring his love for her on his chest, you have some unique situations that other couples don't have to deal with. To make matters worse, unless you have friends or family who have also been involved with a widower, it's hard for them to understand and relate to many of the concerns that come up. The purpose of this book is to help you think through and overcome these one-of-a-kind situations, and to show you that you're not alone.

In addition, this book has two chapters that discuss the best way to deal with breakups, should your relationship with a widower come to an end, and whether or not you should give him a second chance. I hope these chapters will help you hold your head high, find closure, and avoid being burned again.

Whether you're married to a widower, dating one, or in a long-term relationship, this book can help you navigate many of the unique issues you encounter and guide you toward a fulfilling, long-lasting relationship.

Abel Keogh
March 2013

CHAPTER 1

WHAT YOU PERMIT, YOU PROMOTE

WHEN I STARTED DATING JULIANNA, one of the things I learned by our third date was that she wasn't going to tolerate any bad behavior from me just because I lost my wife. She let me know in no uncertain terms that if I was really ready to date again, to open my heart to someone other than my late wife, I needed to treat her like the center of my universe. She would not be made to feel like she was second place. If she felt like I wasn't ready to move on, or that I was simply using her as a placeholder, the relationship would be over.

Julianna's high standards took me by complete surprise. I had recently ended my first serious relationship with a woman I'll call Jennifer. When we started dating, Jennifer didn't set any expectations about how she wanted to be treated or wanted me to behave. If anything, I was allowed to get away with behavior Jennifer probably wouldn't have tolerated from other men simply because I was a recent widower.

For example, after we started dating exclusively, I kept my relationship with Jennifer a secret from my immediate family and close friends. Jennifer knew I hadn't told anyone about her, and though she asked me a couple times when I was going to spread the word, I told her that my friends and family were still grieving and would probably have a hard time seeing me with someone else. I kept the relationship a secret as long as I could and only broke the news a few days before she was scheduled to fly in to visit. Since I lived just down the street from my parents' home at the time, I knew there was no way I could keep her visit from them. I only told them about us because I was *forced* to—not because it was something I *wanted* to do. Had she not flown in to see me, or if I had lived far away from the prying eyes of family and friends, I don't know when, if ever, I would have told anyone about our relationship.

What I didn't realize all those years ago—but Julianna understood very well—was that when you allow a widower to get away with bad or unacceptable behavior through silence or by making excuses for him, you're sanctioning it. Julianna already had plenty of concerns about dating a recent widower. The last thing she wanted was to waste her time in a relationship where she had to compete with a ghost or feel like a replacement. She was only going to seriously date someone who would treat her like a queen, and she wasn't going to make exceptions for me. After setting her expectations, she waited to see if I loved her enough to treat her the way she wanted. Not once did she lower those expectations or allow me to get away with things because of my loss. We've been married for ten years, and her expectations are the same now as they were the day I met her.

Julianna's boundaries forced me to decide how much I valued her and whether or not she was worth pursuing. Had I simply been looking to fill the hole in my heart, the relationship wouldn't have lasted very long, and I would have moved on to someone who would make excuses for me.

On the other hand, Jennifer's permissive attitude taught me that it was perfectly acceptable if I treated her like some dirty little secret. I could play the grief card whenever I said or did something out of line. It was the ultimate "Get out of Jail Free" card, and I'm ashamed to say that I used it every time the opportunity presented itself. Instead of having to explain why I was acting a certain way or hadn't kept my promises or commitments, I could just say I was going through a tough time, and that would be that. End of story.

If Jennifer had put her foot down early on about the secret nature of our relationship, I would have been forced to think about how much being with her really meant to me. Looking back, I believe I would have valued the opinions of my family and close friends over hers, and the relationship never would have become as serious as it did. In the long run, that would have been a good thing because Jennifer deserved someone who wanted what she did: a serious, committed relationship.

If you don't set expectations and boundaries or confront the widower when he steps out of line, you're going to get used and abused. On the other hand, by permitting certain behavior early in the relationship, it's going to be much easier for him to continue to come up with excuses for not changing when things finally reach a breaking point.

One common example of this is when a widower takes his girlfriend into the bedroom he and the late wife shared. Upon entering the room, the girlfriend discovers that there's at least one picture of the late wife hanging on the wall or sitting on the nightstand, and/or the late wife's clothes, toiletries, and other personal items are still where she left them. Instead of feeling like a quiet, private place where they can enjoy an intimate moment together, it feels like they're going to have sex while the late wife watches.

At this point, the girlfriend has a choice to make: She can proceed like everything's okay, even though she feels uncomfortable with all the late wife's things in the room, or she can stop the kissing and the foreplay and tell the widower how uncomfortable she feels. Either way, boundaries and expectations will be set.

By proceeding, she's telling the widower that having photos of the late wife staring at them while they share a passionate moment is okay, even though she probably wouldn't tolerate the photo of an ex-wife or past girlfriend "watching" them if the man was single or divorced. Maybe she's worried that saying no will make the widower think she doesn't love him or it will create an awkward situation. While consenting may avoid an uncomfortable conversation now, she's telling the widower that there are no late-wife boundaries when it comes to the bedroom. It also makes it harder for the widower to take down the photos later when she finally voices her concern about them. She slept with him before without saying a word, so he won't see what an important issue it really is. It gives him a good excuse to drag his feet or see how serious she really is by trying to get her back in the bedroom.

On the other hand, if she says that doing it with the late wife's things everywhere is too uncomfortable or doesn't put her in the mood, she's drawing a line in the sand.

It may be embarrassing to tell the widower you're not sleeping with him while the late wife watches, but life is full of awkward situations where we have to stand up for our values and beliefs. Besides, when you're dating a widower, there are going to be plenty of similar situations down the road. The sooner you can stand up for yourself, the better it will be for your physical, mental, and emotional health.

These uncomfortable moments are a good way to see whether or not the widower is going to respect you. If he does, he'll find a way to put your wants and needs first. He may take the photos down, suggest another room, or say that you should both wait until he's more ready to take this step. A widower who doesn't care about your thoughts and feelings will do everything he can to wear down your resistance. He may say the photos aren't a big deal and that you're overreacting. Or maybe he'll say that if they bother you that much, you should leave. Either way, you'll get a good glimpse of the real man you're dating.

Figure out early what you will and won't tolerate and then set clear boundaries. Widowers who want to move on will try their best to meet your expectations. They may screw up several times along the way, but they'll keep trying to reach the bar you set for them without making excuses as to why they're falling short.

I wasn't always perfect when it came to the expectations Julianna set for me, but at least she could tell I was trying my best. And please note that I never intentionally tried to cross any lines. As things moved forward, she was able to see that I really was the man she thought I was—someone I might not have become had she relaxed her standards.

Even if you've allowed certain behavior to go on for a period of time, it's never too late to have a heart-to-heart conversation with the widower to let him know what's expected of him. You just need to explain in a very loving manner why you've permitted the behavior and why you're setting new boundaries. The key to making this work is to be strong and firm in your resolution and to not be afraid of ending things if he tries to lower the bar. There's not a man on earth—widower, single, or divorced—that's worth settling for.

∿

RAQUEL'S STORY

I first met my widower approximately twenty-two years ago through his wife. She and I worked at the same hospital in the same department. They were married for thirty years and had a near-perfect marriage. In

ABEL KEOGH ⌒ 11

June of 2011, I attended her funeral. She died of pancreatic cancer approximately fifteen weeks following diagnosis.

As I stood waiting to be ushered to my seat, my widower came toward me and gave me a hug. We had not seen each other for nearly twenty years. As Christmas drew near, I was thinking about him and gave him a call. We started dating immediately, and in March we began living together in the home he had shared with his late wife.

I soon realized that her pictures were not going to come down anytime soon. There was an obituary on the fridge as well. I felt as though our future was buried in the past. I felt he wanted both of us, and that I was not number one in his present life. He was happy to live this way, but I could not. I blamed it on my insecurities at first, but realized that I needed to be the special person in his life today.

Because we were involved only six months following the late wife's death, we went through a lot of firsts. A month after I moved into his home, he held a concert in his late wife's honor to raise money for pancreatic cancer. He sang love songs to her for over two hours.

He sang those songs again from time to time after the service, and that hurt, but I did get better at handling it. We also had the first Mother's Day, the anniversary of her death, and his oldest daughter's wedding. I also attended the annual reunion of the late wife's family. They were so good to me. I understood that naturally they wished the late wife could be there instead of me.

We had three counseling sessions, at which time the counselor suggested moving the photos to another room. My widower made a shrine in another room. This still bothered me, and following that, he told me that I was being disrespectful. I'd known her and worked with her, and would never be disrespectful. He expected that the bookshelf would have a picture of him and his late wife on one side, and one of us on the other. I know that I was compared to her perfection as a cook and housekeeper, the way I did my makeup, hair, and dress, and in other ways I don`t want to imagine. He told me that in the relationship prior to me, he saw his late wife`s face during sex. My feeling was that if he did anything nice for me, he felt he was being disrespectful to the late wife. He could not hold hands with me, as he had not done so with her.

We never did recover. He was angry that I wanted him to put the pictures in a special place such as an album or memory box (which he considered hidden), and his attitude toward me changed. He told me the reality: I would always live in the shadow of his late. I moved out. I was always a guest in the home—my widower was not ready to move forward. A widow friend tells me how much difference one more year will make, but it is too late for us.

CHAPTER 2

THE ONE THING YOU SHOULD NEVER TALK ABOUT WITH YOUR WIDOWER

IF YOU'VE READ *Dating a Widower, Marrying a Widower* or any of my Widower Wednesday columns, you know that I'm a big proponent of learning how to communicate. In fact, there's a chapter later in this book giving suggestions on how you can open the lines of communication. The majority of widower-related situations can be solved or improved simply by letting each other know how certain words, actions, and behaviors affect you and your relationship. If you can't learn to talk to each other openly and honestly, there is little chance your relationship will succeed.

That being said, there is one thing you should never talk about: His sex life with the late wife. It doesn't matter if you're curious about what they did in the bedroom together or if he wants to brag about his virility. When details of their sex life emerge, they will make you either feel like you can't measure up to the late wife in bed, or they will blemish whatever romantic image you have of the widower. That knowledge will have long-lasting, negative consequences and can permanently scar your relationship. Let me give you two examples that recently reached my inbox.

In the first, a woman asked the widower to tell her about the most sexually adventurous thing he'd ever done with the late wife. The widower smiled and told her about the time his wife invited a female friend of hers into bed with the two of them, and then proceeded to graphically detail the threesome. The woman was never able to look at the widower the same way again. The knowledge of his past escapade bothered her so much, that she seriously thought of ending the relationship, because she had a hard time being with someone who could take his marriage vows so lightly. To add salt to the wound, the friend of the wife who had engaged in the threesome was someone in town that she knew, which made it hard to attend certain parties and business functions, because that person was someone she'd eventually bump into.

In the second example, a woman asked her widower about how their sex life compared with his sex life with the late wife. After listening to several detailed stories from the widower about the passionate lovemaking sessions he and the late wife had enjoyed together, the woman left the house with tears running down her cheeks, convinced that she'd never be able to measure up to the late wife in the bedroom.

I could cite dozens of other emails or threads that have circulated on discussion boards about this subject. In every case, learning what the widower and the late wife enjoyed during their most intimate moments was never a good thing. In the first example above, the threesome revelation ended up being the crack that eventually ended the couple's relationship. The second couple was able to patch things up and move on, but it took a lot of time for those wounds to heal.

Discussing the widower's past sex life (or yours, for that matter) is just as poisonous as having photos of the late spouse all over the widower's home, or having the late wife's clothing and other personal items lying untouched in her closets and drawers. Intimate moments between two people should stay between them. Period. No exceptions. What the widower and his late wife did together in the bedroom has no bearing whatsoever on your current relationship. Instead of thinking what he did with the late wife, concentrate on what the two of you share during those times and how you can make it stronger and better.

If the widower wants to bring up the subject, shush him gently and let him know that those things should stay between the two of them, and that you expect that whatever private moments you two share will stay between the two of you. If he loves and respects you, he'll zip his lips and drop the subject.

You can never unhear something, and whatever he tells you will put images in your mind that you'll never be able to shake. Worst of all, they'll pop into your mind at the least opportune times. A relationship should be one of two hearts—not three or more. There's no faster way to kill your sex life than to have the late wife in the bedroom with you—even if it's just as thoughts in your mind.

As one final plea not to do this, I'll share a personal story: Early in my marriage to Julianna, I let something slip about my sex life with the late wife. I thought it would be a fun way to get Julianna in the mood for something different. Instead it had the opposite effect in a very bad way. Even though it was a small thing, for a long time, it made Julianna feel that in that way, she couldn't measure up. Yes, we worked through it, and our love life is fine now, thank-you-very-much, but it was an issue we wouldn't have had to deal with if only I had kept my big mouth shut.

Learn from my mistake and the two stories shared in this chapter. Knowledge of their sex life won't do a thing to strengthen the love you have for each other. Your relationship will be stronger and better when you concentrate on each other's wants and needs and leave the past out of your bedroom.

⌒

KAREN'S STORY

The tendency is, at first, to let him talk because you think the more you know about his relationship with his late wife, the better equipped you will be in your relationship. No, no, no! Did your mother ever tell you not to kiss and tell? Well, don't kiss and listen, either! The stories I've heard about my husband's sex life with his late wife have come back to haunt me in intimate moments.

The memories I've allowed him to share have come to mind at the most unfortunate times and have sent me into a downward spiral emotionally. It's very difficult to take those thoughts captive and put them out of my mind. It's much easier to stop him from sharing those stories than to try to keep them out of my mind when something triggers such thoughts. I didn't need to know what she liked or how she liked it. I'm not *her*! I don't need to know even little details, like which side of the bed she slept on, because those things are not relevant to *our* relationship. I cannot imagine why he needs to tell me those things. My widower's late wife was nineteen when they got married, and I was fifty-four when I married him. It's not fair to hear him talk about "screwing like rabbits" like he did when he married his nineteen-year-old late wife. I was pretty hot at nineteen too, but that ship has sailed!

You know that TLC show Sister Wives? That's what it feels like when he talks about sex with the former wife. It's like I'm a sister wife, only he doesn't have to go next door to visit her, because she lives in his head, in our house, in our bedroom! I wish I had known to stop the stories before they were told, because they're a lot for me to overcome. I can't be in charge of his memories, but I can be in charge of how much of them he shares with me. Sometimes I have to tell him to stop.

EDIE'S STORY

My widower and I are best friends and confidants, which is a blessing most of the time, but other times it's a curse. I have never felt the need to share any of the intimate details of the seventeen years with my ex-husband, but for some reason, my widower feels the need to share intimate details about him and his late wife.

I learned early on in our relationship that his late wife had very large breasts. They were so big that she couldn't find a bra at Victoria's Secret. She had considered having them reduced but never did, and I think it may have been because they were one of the things that attracted him to her so much in the first place. I was very thin when we started dating, so I was at the mercy of the all-mighty push-up to give myself curves. I felt as though I could never compete in that area. I have gained a few pounds and have a few more curves, but I still picture the late wife as Jessica Rabbit. How can I compare to that?

We had been dating almost a year before I moved in. My widower and his son went through the garage to sort and throw out items, many of which were the late wife's. My widower felt the need to tell me that one of the items he ran across was a "Clone-a-Willy" that his late wife had made. I had no idea you could actually take a mold of your significant other's private parts and make a sex toy out of it. Though I appreciate my widower's "asset," did I really need to know how much the late wife enjoyed it too?

The one thing that always sticks in my mind, however, is something my widower feels necessary to discuss every couple of months. I think he's told me the story at least six times. It goes like this: When his late wife was in hospice, and two days from her passing, she asked that he make love to her one last time. She was fragile, so he was afraid of hurting her. When he tells the story, it's quite detailed. Now I can't get the picture of them doing it out of my mind. I don't know why he feels the need to share that moment with me. It makes me feel very uncomfortable. It's a sweet story, but I hope that if I pass on before he does, he'll have a little more discretion in sharing his last experiences with his next girlfriend. There are some things I don't want others to know.

CHAPTER 3

EVENTS THAT COMMEMORATE THE LATE WIFE

THE OTHER DAY, I found a flier on my front door announcing a 5K walk/run in honor of a local woman who had recently lost her fight with cancer. The purpose of the race was to help raise money for a charitable organization that funds cancer research. While events like this were rare when my late wife died, holding charitable fundraisers or starting foundations to honor a deceased family member are things that have had a huge uptick in popularity over the last decade.

While I don't have a problem with charity runs or starting a foundation in a loved one's honor, these events can cause a lot of stress and strain for the new woman in the widower's life. In fact, fundraisers, foundation meetings, and other charitable events can make it seem like his life is centered around the memory of the late wife instead of looking to the future and embracing his current relationship.

Everyone has different ways of grieving and moving on. For some, running a race in the late wife's memory can be therapeutic, helping a widower close a certain chapter of his life. If the event raises money for a local charity, it may help the widower feel like he's preventing others from losing a spouse and experiencing the same grief he's endured. For others, however, these kinds of events focus on the widower's loss and hinder him from successfully moving on. They can do just as much harm as constant trips to the cemetery or shrines or photographs of the late wife in his home.

It can be hard to let the widower know that an often good and worthwhile activity is driving a wedge between the two of you. Because the event is focused on the late wife, any complaint or concerns might be taken as an attack on the late wife or an act of jealousy. Therefore, it's important to tread carefully when broaching the subject to avoid any misunderstandings about your concern. Before you decide to talk to the widower about the event, think about the following five points.

1. **Decide how much his participation really bothers you.** Some people are okay with a widower participating in events or spending time with a foundation or other charitable cause. Others have a hard time with it. There's no right or wrong way to feel about this. What you need to figure out is how big of a deal it really is to you. Is it something you'd be okay with him doing once or multiple days a year? At what point would it become too much? Do you know what his plans are now and in the future when it comes to participating in similar events? Only you know the answer to these questions, and first and foremost, you need to decide if this is a battle worth fighting.

2. **Does the event affect the widower's attitude?** A good way to determine whether these events are harmful or helpful for the widower's quest to move on is seeing what his mood is like in the days

preceding the event, on the day of the event, and a day or two after. If he's moody, depressed, uptight, or wallows in the past, then odds are that whatever he's participating in isn't helping him open his heart to you. However, if the widower acts more or less like his normal self and is still able to keep you at the center of his life, then maybe his participation isn't necessarily a bad thing.

3. **Participation in these events usually declines**. Widowers are most active in these charitable events within the first two or three years after the late wife dies. As time passes, and they become more involved in the new chapter of their lives, participation in these events usually declines and eventually stops altogether. If you're with a widower who has only been widowed a couple of years, this might not even be an issue in a few more years.

4. **Don't feel obligated to participate**. Many times, wives and girlfriends of widowers feel pressured to either participate in or volunteer for these events. While there's nothing wrong with being part of the event if it's something you want to do, you shouldn't

feel any obligation to help out. If you have no desire to participate, lovingly explain to the widower that it's not something you can be part of at this time, wish him much success at the event, then go out and have a fun day by yourself or with friends.

5. **Don't ask him NOT to participate**. Even if you feel the event isn't good for your relationship, the one thing you shouldn't do is ask the widower *not* to participate. Explain how you feel if you think that will help, but choosing to participate now and in the future is something the widower needs to decide for himself. If he feels that you pressured him, step back. Otherwise he's going to resent you for it, and it will come back to bite you at the least convenient time. The widower needs to give up the event voluntarily because he values your feelings and your relationship. Also, it's important to keep in mind that it may be hard for him to back out of commitments he made months earlier. If this is the case, he should be able to decide whether to participate in future events.

Only you can judge whether these events are stopping the two of you from moving forward. The best thing you can do to overcome this and other obstacles is to develop solid communication skills so you can talk openly and honestly with each other without one or both of you getting upset. In the end, this issue is between you and the widower. It is my hope that you won't let anything come between the two of you.

─── ∾ ───

LUCY'S STORY

When I started dating Rick, he and his two daughters were gearing up for a run to help raise money to fight breast cancer. At first I thought this was a nice way to pay tribute to his late wife and others who had died from the disease. I even drove them to the run that morning and supported them as they did the race. But at the time, we were casually dating. We didn't get serious until a few months later. I didn't give the run a second thought until almost a year later, when they began preparing for the next one.

Suddenly it seemed like their lives revolved around

the run and the late wife. At first I was okay with it, but it got harder and harder to bear as time went by. I stopped feeling like part of their family and more like a stranger who just happened to spend time with Rick. The girls wanted me to help make fliers and do other things to get ready, and I agreed, even though I felt I should take a step back and not get involved.

Then one day, I woke up and dreaded going over to their house. I couldn't stand to see the pictures and everything else that was out for the race. I called him at work later that day and told him we needed to have an important talk that night. I was nervous the rest of the day and thought that this conversation would sink our relationship.

We met up, and with tears in my eyes, I told him I couldn't help out with the race anymore, but that I supported them running it. Rick was quiet for a minute, and then told me he didn't realize how much the race was affecting me, but that he could see how it would be hard. He said they didn't have to run the race, and that our relationship was more important. I told him they had already promised to run it, and they should keep their commitments.

The day of the race came. Afterward, they all came over to my house and had lunch. We had a good time, and it seemed like things were back to normal. Time passed, and our relationship grew stronger. This year they decided as a family not to run the race. They do other things to remember their mother, like visit her grave. I'm fine with that and the few other things they do to remember her.

Having that conversation with Rick was one of the hardest things I've ever done, but I'm glad I did it. It opened the lines of communication and changed our lives for the better. The experience taught us both that we shouldn't let events or memories of the past get in the way of love. Things are moving forward with Rick, and I couldn't be happier.

CHAPTER 4

THE LATE WIFE'S FACEBOOK PAGE AND OTHER ONLINE MEMORIALS

WHILE PHOTOGRAPHS of the late wife or shrines in the widower's home are, unfortunately, something many women have to deal with, it's become more common for memorials to move from the real world to the virtual one. Generally, online shrines take place in the form of the late wife's Facebook page, but they also include websites dedicated to the life of the deceased. Even though they only exist in cyberspace, these shrines can be just as damaging to a relationship as any real-world one.

Before I get too deep into this, let me be clear: I

don't have a problem with keeping the Facebook page of someone up after he or she passes on, or of creating some type of memorial website. My concern with them is the same one I have with real-world shrines: they make it easy for the widower to focus on the past and what he has lost instead of the blessings and relationships he enjoys today. In our connected world of smartphones and laptops, all it takes is the push of a button to post a favorite photo of the late wife or to write a sentence or two about her that the entire world—which the widower's girlfriend or current wife can see.

In most cases, the existence of the Facebook page or online memorial isn't what causes the strife and contention. Rather, problems arise when the widower adds photographs to the page, posts regular comments on it about how much he misses her, and spends excessive amounts of time on the page or site dedicated to her.

So what's the best way to deal with online shrines? Do the same as you would if the shrine were in the widower's home.

First, you've got to be able to talk about it. Next time the widower posts a comment that causes you to question where his heart is, don't stew over it, trying to figure out some secret meaning to his words. Give him a call, or, better yet, bring it up next time you see him. The conversation doesn't have to be confrontational. Just stating what you noticed and how it made you feel is a good way to get started. Discuss it and get it over with. It's easy to misinterpret someone's intentions online. Just because the widower shares a memory or says something about missing her doesn't mean that he doesn't love you. You need to keep in mind how he treats you in the real world too.

Second, Facebook can serve as a surprising window to the soul. If he's always posting photos of his past online, but not mentioning you or posting anything about you or your relationship, that's a red flag. This is pretty much the same as keeping his house full of photos of himself and the late wife, but not hanging up photos of you or hiding you from friends and family. If the widower really loves you, he won't have a hard time letting the world—even Facebook friends he barely knows—know that he loves you too.

Finally, just like you're not under any obligation to spend time in a home, room, or with a person who memorializes the late wife to the point where you feel uncomfortable, there's no reason you should feel required to "friend" the late wife's Facebook page, "like" her memorial page, or add any of her friends and family. There's no point in getting on Facebook or spending time online if it's going to make you uncomfortable or strain your relationship.

At some point, the widower will have to decide what he values more—a relationship with a Facebook page, or one with a real person. You'll never be able to compete with a ghost that exists online or in the real world. If he chooses the online version, count your lucky stars that you figured it out before things got too serious.

JANEEN'S STORY

I dread February. Why do I dread a month with a holiday requiring little more than a Kay Jeweler's catalog? February is also the birth and death month of my husband's late wife.

After we were married, my husband and I started a

Facebook page to share a memorial scholarship fund in the late wife's name which was established the year she died. We thought we could expand the outreach and raise more money for the scholarship through social media. It is a wonderful scholarship, a fantastic memorial, and it was a great idea. And it ended there. Social media can be a great way of reaching people, but it can also be the devil. Suddenly, friend requests from everyone all over the state flooded in, friends of friends joining in on decade-late condolences and asking how my husband was doing.

Something happens when people sign in to Facebook. Their filter disappears, and they completely lose all sense of boundaries. Though some people genuinely cared how my husband was doing, many posted things they would never dare say to me face-to-face. They also gladly memorialized the dead for infinity— even if they barely knew her.

Then February rolled around. People started to wish my sister wife a happy birthday on the page. It was as if they challenged each other to see who could come up with the most ridiculous posts. None of it had anything to do with the scholarship, and very little had to do with her or her birthday. Later the same month, the scholarship page became an homage to all the loved ones lost over the years by every friend of the page. People threw around dates and death stories; the page developed twisted, tangled warts, and the content couldn't have gotten any further from the original intent.

My husband took the lead in support of our marriage and swept the page clean. He posted a reminder about the intent of the page, and we kept going.

Then the new year arrived. I awoke on the late wife's death day to notifications of all sorts. Her sister had created some sort of PowerPoint set to dreary music with over 100 photos. Not only had she posted this video montage on the scholarship page, but she had posted it to my personal Facebook page! My private, secret world, free from my sister wife, had been invaded, ambushed overnight, as I slept. I felt so violated, so attacked, so betrayed.

My husband deleted the video and called the creator. I "unliked" the scholarship page to keep myself sane, to protect my own world. It had taken on a life of its own, sometimes too wacky for me to cope with. I can support the memory of the late wife without sup-porting the mania of the people behind it.

Hubby can't always understand how I feel, but I know that no matter what, we are there for each other, figuring it out together, through tears and laughter and WTF.

CHAPTER 5

WHAT TO DO ABOUT MEMORIAL TATTOOS

TATTOOS ARE NO LONGER the domain of just soldiers, bikers, or carnival workers. They adorn the bodies of professional athletes, actors, and CEOs. As their popularity has increased, so has the number of widowers who get a memorial tattoo after losing a spouse. While a memorial tattoo isn't a bad thing in and of itself, it can cause problems between a widower and his new girlfriend. As one emailer wrote, "I have a hard time wanting to make love to my widower when I see the heart tattoo with his late wife's initials every time he takes off his shirt."

Not everyone is bothered by the presence of

memorial tattoos. But for those who are, here are three suggestions to help you decide if the tattoo is a deal breaker, or if you should broach the subject of having it removed.

1. **Don't take the tattoo personally.** Most widowers get memorial tattoos within weeks or months of the late wife's passing, when dating someone else or having a serious relationship again is usually the last thing on the widower's mind. In that context, the tattoo isn't there to spite you or make you feel like second place; rather, it's the result of an emotional decision that happened before you came into his life. The only time you should take it personally is if he gets it *after* you're in a serious relationship, and without your knowledge or consent. In that case, there may be a question as to whether he's ready to open his heart to someone else.

2. **Decide how much the tattoo really bothers you.** Examine the relationship as a whole and decide if the tattoo is a deal breaker. Does the widower treat you how you expect to be treated? Can you see a lifelong relationship with him? What really bothers

you about the tattoo? Do you have to look at it all the time, or just when you're intimate? Do you feel like it's the equivalent of having a photograph of the late wife in the living room or bedroom? Knowing in advance if this is an issue you want to fight can prevent a lot of unnecessary arguments before they start. It's okay to ask for the tattoo to be removed if it bothers you enough. However, look at all the other facets of the relationship before deciding if it really is a deal breaker.

3. **Tattoos become "wallpaper" to widowers.** You may find the tattoo distracting, but that doesn't mean that every time the widower sees the tattoo, he pines after the late wife and wishes she were alive. Most men don't think like that. After the tattoo loses its novelty, it generally becomes part of their body. They go through their day and usually don't think anything of it unless someone points it out or asks them what it means. A good way to determine if the tattoo is a distraction for him is to note how often he stares at it or brings it up in conversation. If he's treating you like number one

and doing everything he can to open his heart to you, odds are that the tattoo, or what it symbolizes, isn't on his mind.

Should you decide that the tattoo is too much to bear, talk to the widower about it in such a way that doesn't come across as jealousy of the late wife or their past relationship. No one expects a widower to erase his past, and asking him to remove a tattoo can sound like exactly that. Be sure he knows that it's not about removing the past, but making you feel that you now have the first position in his heart.

Keep in mind that tattoo removal can be a long and painful process, and many people don't want to go through that ordeal. If the widower wants to honor your wishes but doesn't want to go through the removal process, the two of you might want to consider a couple of alternatives:

- A modification to the tattoo. Is there some way the tattoo can be altered so it changes or obscures the original meaning—something that you can both be happy with? It may be worth a trip to a tattoo parlor to see what options are available.

- Suggest that the widower get another tattoo, one that symbolizes *your* relationship. Maybe you can get matching tattoos or something else that shows your commitment to each other.

In the end, this is a personal decision you and the widower need to make.

Whatever you choose, be sure to weigh all of the pros and cons before asking him to remove it, or decide if you can accept it being a permanent part of your relationship.

ᐤ

JANA'S STORY

I was not one of those girlfriends who had to deal with a memorial tattoo permanently etched on their widower's body while he was in the throes of grief, certain he would never love again. My widower arrived in my life unadorned, and, in fact, a little mystified at the whole trend of permanently inking significant symbols into one's skin. I was the one who encouraged my widower to get a tattoo. It's a suggestion I now regret making, as the results are a painful reminder of how selfish and hurtful memorial tattoos can be.

It started when my widower hurt his shoulder and sought chiropractic treatment, which included extensive taping of his shoulder. I told him that the black tape strips on his shoulder attracted me, as they emphasized his broad, muscular features. I told him I would like it very much if he got a tattoo on his shoulder. I spent an entire day researching tattoos and came up with the idea that we should use our zodiac signs with some tribal outline to fill in as a basis for the design. He decided to add his two children's signs as well. A local tattoo artist spent a week bringing the idea to life.

Then we had a horrible fight. I don't even recall what it was about, but my widower decided it was significant enough to remove my sign from the tattoo. I was heartbroken. I told him it was insensitive to do such permanent thing to his body when he was angry, but he got the tattoo with the new design despite my objections.

He ended up getting two tattoos, and both were something very different than either of us had imagined. Our relationship went from bad to worse, and soon after, I moved out. Months went by. I found my-self again and dated many wonderful men who lifted my self-esteem but who could never replace the wid-ower in my heart. My widower begged me to come back, and I resisted as long as I could, but I eventually decided to give him a second chance.

Things improved, and we ended up getting en-gaged a few months later. One night I mentioned the zodiac tattoo. I told him it bothered me greatly that I wasn't included in the final design. I said, "At least I like the other tattoo." Then he let the cat out of the bag: The tattoo on the shoulder on which I rested my head at night was actually a memorial tattoo for his late wife. I was dumbfounded.

I ran out the door in tears. I avoided his phone calls for a day so I had time to think things through. It has been a month since he told me about the tattoo, and the shock has lessened, but not the hurt. I wouldn't be bothered so much if the tattoo wasn't so much "in my face" or if he had gotten it before we met, but I feel that he got the tattoo deliberately to hurt me. I still can't stand to look at it.

～

TAMI'S STORY

One day out of the blue, my widower told me he was going to get a memorial tattoo on his arm to commemorate his late wife. I freaked out. I don't have anything against tattoos, but I didn't think I could handle him getting one after we were in a committed relationship. Nor could I handle seeing his late wife's name every time I looked at his arm.

Finally I got the courage to bring the subject up. I calmly approached him and told him we needed to have a serious talk, that this was important and perhaps something that could end our relationship. I simply told him that I could not live with the tattoo he was planning, and where he was planning on putting it. I didn't need a constant reminder that he had lost his wife. I also told him that if he was trying to move on, he didn't need to see something like that on his arm either.

Much to my surprise, he agreed.

He said that the tattoo was something he had talked about getting since her death, but for some reason was never able to go through with. When it came right down to it, he didn't want to permanently put anything sad or negative on himself. He also said that my feelings mattered to him very much, and that he wouldn't do anything that would hurt me or cause me to leave him. He'd known when he first brought it up that I was very upset, so he had decided not to do it anyway.

I did tell him that he should get a tattoo that would be a gentle reminder of her—just not one that was an in-your-face reminder of his past. She loved dragons, so I told him to get a really beautiful dragon tattoo on his back. He loved that idea.

I am not really against him memorializing her with a tattoo. It's just that I don't want to look at her name or something like that. What he had been planning was major and depressing. Now he'll have something we can both live with.

TIFFANY'S STORY

Mike and I have known each other since 1994, when we worked together. We became friends quickly and easily. When I got married in 1995, he and his late wife were at my wedding. They were a lovely couple. I ended up leaving that job later that year and losing touch with him until we reconnected on Facebook soon after his wife died in 2010. It was really nice catching up with him. We shared many personal and heartfelt feelings about our relationships with his deceased wife and my ex-husband. We had a well-grounded friendship, which was all we saw at the time.

He had told me that he thought of getting the tattoo. He loved her and would always love her. He asked my advice. He told me that my opinion really mattered to him. My thoughts were this: She had been a living, breathing human being that was a significant part of his life for about 20 years. She would always matter to him. She was the mother of his children. What a great tribute a tattoo would be to a fantastic woman. Who would I be to stop him? He had my support. It wasn't until well after getting the tattoo that we started dating.

The tattoo was drawn by their son, which is a picture of their wedding bands intertwined, plus their anniversary date and initials, with the words Together Forever. The tattoo takes up the whole of his upper left arm. I am not mad about it. I don't have a right to be. I don't think he will ever regret getting it, nor should he. Regardless of where we are in our relationship, I know that eventually, he wants to be with her again. That doesn't bother me as long as I'm with him too.

If there's one thing I've learned from dating a widower, it's this: The tattoo has nothing to do with me. It doesn't change his feelings for me. It is a symbol of his love for her; it's nothing personal. I'm sure there will be some way he will symbolize his love for me. Maybe it will be a tattoo. Maybe it will be something else. I'm confident in knowing that he does love me. You have to be confident in your relationship with your widower and in his love for you. If the tattoo bothers you that much, then walk away, because that part of him is there to stay.

CHAPTER 6

TAKING IT TO THE NEXT LEVEL: A LEAP OF FAITH

BY THE TIME this book is published, Julianna and I will have celebrated our tenth wedding anniversary. When we got married, there were some who thought the relationship wouldn't last a year. I had only been widowed for fifteen months when we exchanged vows—not enough time to move on, by some people's standards. And at the time we got married, we had only been in a serious, committed relationship for about seven months—a length of time some would consider too short. But we didn't listen to the naysayers. Instead, we followed our guts and took that leap of faith all couples must take when they start a new life together.

Even though we both felt like we were doing the right thing, there was always a chance that things wouldn't work out. The night before we tied the knot, I stared at the ceiling, wondering what the future would hold for us. What if I woke up one day and decided I had made a mistake? What if Julianna threw her hands up and said she couldn't take being the wife of a widower anymore? What would happen if one of us contracted a life-threatening illness and died? What if we made bad financial decisions and lost everything? My mind raced through a thousand other scenarios of bad things that could happen, and for one brief instant, I wondered if I had made the right decision.

Then my mind wandered back to my first marriage. It ended sooner than we had anticipated and in a horrible, bloody way. Toward the end of our marriage, there were some truly dark moments, but despite the way things turned out, I never once regretted marrying my late wife, because I loved her, and it was the right thing to do. So why was I so concerned about what the future held for me and Julianna?

Then I started thinking of all the good things that might happen if we got married. I thought about how nice it would be to wake up every morning with the woman I loved at my side. There would be the opportunity of having children and raising a family together, and chances to hug and hold each other when we had bad days. I could also be with someone who made me a better person. The list of good things kept getting longer and longer, and I realized that whatever the future held, I was doing the right thing by taking Julianna to be my wife.

The next day, Julianna and I pledged our love to each other for this life and for all eternity. I've never looked back on that day with the least bit of regret.

So why am I sharing this? Over the years, I've read emails and talked with widowers and girlfriends of widowers who are madly in love with each other but have just enough uncertainty that they can't bring themselves to take that next step. So many what-ifs keep popping up that they take a step back every time one little problem arises or a seed of doubt is planted in their minds.

Marriage is the beginning of a new life. Whether you're marrying a widower, someone who's divorced, or a bachelor, you can only see so far into the future.

There are never any guarantees about what will happen one, five, or ten years down the road. Sometimes spouses make unfortunate choices that can destroy their marriages. Other times, life events like unemployment, illness, or financial hardships come up. Trials and tribulations are simply part of life. They will come whether we're married or single. What you need to decide is if the person you're with is the one you want by your side when those problems and challenges arise.

Despite the uncertainty, if you know something to be right, you've got to take that step forward, even when you can't tell exactly where that step will take you. More often than not, when I've had to step into the darkness, I've prayed hard that everything would work out in the end. Taking that leap of faith after you've thought things through is better than living in a constant state of worry about what *might* happen.

My marriage to Julianna has far exceeded both of our expectations. I've never been happier. Even when unexpected and challenging times have presented themselves, I've discovered that I can get through them better with Julianna at my side. Ten years ago, it would have been easy for either of us to let our doubts, fears, and concerns get in the way. Had we done that, I doubt either of us would be as happy as we are right now.

If there aren't any major red flags in your relationship, don't let unfounded doubts and worries hold you back from taking that next step—whatever it may be—with your widower. You'll face unexpected challenges on your journey. But if you can see him being there for you, and you doing the same for him, what are you waiting for? If your gut tells both of you that this is the right thing to do, the only choice you have is to hold each other's hand and take that step forward together.

HEATHER'S STORY

I was the divorced mother of a six-year-old son when I started dating my now-husband, Scott.

Scott and I were dear friends. I met him through his wife Ana in 2003. Ana and I carpooled and worked together. We also hung out afterhours. Scott is a professional musician and educator. When Ana was alive, he played in a fun band, and she and I often traipsed around town, following his band and enjoying time together.

Then Ana was diagnosed with Stage IV cancer in July of 2004. Everything ground to a halt.

I was one of the many who loved Ana dearly. Her death was tragic beyond words, and we were all left mourning our loss when she passed in April of 2005.

As expected, Scott was terribly lonely. He did awkward things, like come to my house, sit on the couch, and say nothing, just watching my son and me play and eat dinner. Our relationship at this point was still just a shaky friendship, with really no rules on how to progress or what to say to each other without Ana to broker the conversation.

Eventually he opened up about his loneliness, and an "affair" he'd had with someone he met online (but never in person), whom he'd talked to while Ana was sick. He talked about how he felt and how much he realized he didn't know about dating. It had been thirteen years of marriage. She was thirty-seven when she died. He was thirty-six.

Life has myriad relationships that take on different forms, and our love grew organically from our conversations. He felt he had to rebuild his life, build new dreams, and find his own reality. I wanted to help, but as our feelings for each other developed, we realized I couldn't really help—not without being biased or having an opinion.

Was it too soon for him to build a life with someone else? Had he dated enough? What would our family and friends think? What would her friends do if they saw us together? I was a relatively new friend, and she had some friends who probably would have resented him.

My son and I showed up at a gig for his band. Another fun Saturday night was in motion. Then I noticed another woman with him at the gig. I had no idea he was dating. He had every right to, but I thought he was telling me everything. The moment was awkward, and he spent a long time on his date. They talked. They might have kissed. I have no idea.

And then it happened. At 9:00 a.m. the next morning he called and started crying. He said he was in love with me, but that he didn't know what to do about it, because he was worried his feelings might be masked with loneliness, pain, and shared memories of Ana.

He'd wanted to try something new, something fresh and outside his past. He liked the new feeling, the lack of shared history, but he also said dating new women made him even lonelier, because he realized how much he wouldn't be able to share.

In a way, our memories, our laughter, and our stories of Ana keep her more alive. This is less important for me than it is for him, but it healed both of us over time. The way it is now, she's still with us. Her mother visits, since Ana was an only child, and we have embraced her as part of our family and share our time with her delicately and with compassion.

There will be more challenges, but I don't regret taking the step to marry Scott. Being married to a widower has some special perks. He loves life and celebrates with me as often as he can. We take vacations and live each day to the fullest. When we laugh, we laugh hard, and when we cry, we cry together.

CHAPTER 7

5 TIPS TO IMPROVE COMMUNICATION WITH YOUR WIDOWER

MANY YEARS AGO, I was talking to a friend at a party when we somehow got on the topic of marriage. She mentioned she was envious that Julianna and I could talk openly about my past marriage and life when the topic came up. When I asked why she felt that way, she looked around to make sure no one else was listening and said in a hushed tone, "I don't even know why my husband's first marriage ended in divorce."

I was too stunned to reply. I couldn't believe she had been married to someone for nearly five years without knowing why his first marriage had ended. I asked if she thought that might be important information to know. She paused before answering and said, "I've always wanted to know, but I worry about opening old wounds and causing problems."

Unfortunately, my friend isn't alone. Many couples face similar challenges when it comes to being able to communicate with each other. And it's not only big issues like the one my friend had, but small, day-to-day issues as well. It's challenging to learn how to communicate effectively with your partner, but it's a vital skill to have if your relationship is to have any chance of long-term success.

Love only goes so far. The only reason Julianna and I have been able to make our relationship and marriage last this long is that we learned to talk about our issues. Once we were able to talk about my past and her concerns, it helped build a solid foundation that allowed us to address other non-widower concerns that came up later.

You both need to feel comfortable talking about his past (when appropriate), any words or actions that are making you feel like number two, issues surrounding his or your children, the late wife's family, and other non-widower issues like finances, sex, employment, and countless other things that come up in any relationship. If you can't reach this point, there will always be unresolved issues and tensions slowly chipping away at the foundation of the relationship you've worked so hard to build.

Because every relationship is unique, I can't tell you the best way to open the communication channels with your widower. However, short of writing an entire book on the subject, here are five tips and tricks that can help you open up the channels of communication and avoid some of the biggest mistakes I see come up over and over again in my inbox and on discussion boards.

1. **Pick up the phone.** Don't try to solve or discuss important problems via text messaging, instant messaging, or email. At the very least, pick up the phone. Preferably, plan a time where you can have a face-to-face conversation without interruption. Electronic communication is fast and convenient, but it does a poor job conveying body language, facial expressions, and vocal tone, which help us understand what others are really saying. When

important issues arise, avoid communication tools that can quickly turn minor issues into major misunderstandings and fights.

2. **Don't forget the Late-Wife Factor.** To have had a successful relationship with the late wife, the widower had to learn the best way to communicate with *her*. But unless you're an exact clone of the woman he lost, he has to learn how to communicate with *you*. It can be rather challenging for a widower to put those old habits he developed for the late wife to the side and learn new ones, but it can be done if the widower really wants the relationship to blossom. For example, my late wife and Julianna have very different ways of talking and expressing their opinions. Krista had a loud, boisterous, and vivacious personality. Julianna, on the other hand, is quiet and shy. When Julianna and I were first dating, I tried to solve issues the same way I would have solved them with Krista, instead of adapting problem-solving skills to fit Julianna's personality. As you can imagine, this caused quite a few misunderstandings and arguments when we were first

together. In order to solve relationship issues, I had to learn how to talk to Julianna, and she had to learn when I was "talking to Krista" instead of talking to her. So keep in mind that the widower may be doing his best to talk to you, but that he simply needs to develop new habits and techniques.

3. **Not everything is about the late wife.** Factors like the widower's personality and family history have a lot to do with the way he's learned to communicate with others. Consequently, when you're having trouble talking about widower-related things, it doesn't always have to do with him being a widower. Learning about his past and family history can go a long way toward explaining how he communicates and interacts with others.

4. **It doesn't happen overnight.** It took almost a year after Julianna and I met before we both felt comfortable talking about my past and other issues that arise in our life. Fortunately, we both saw that we were making progress in that area, and we kept moving forward despite the occasional setback. Even though we've been married ten years, there

are still days when we have misunderstandings or other difficulties arise because one or both of us stumble when it comes to letting the other person know about our wants and needs. There's not a couple alive who can perfectly communicate with one another all the time. There are bound to be stumbling blocks along the road. What you want to see in your relationship, however, is progress. As the two of you move forward together, any communication issues should become less frequent and less severe.

5. **It takes two to make it work.** Communication is a two-way street. It's going to take effort from both of you if there's any hope of learning how to talk openly and honestly with each other. You can give it your all, but if the widower isn't trying his best, the results are going to be one-sided and disastrous.

Even if your communication with your widower has been less than stellar up to now, it's not too late to start over and learn how best to communicate with each other. It's been many years since my conversation with my friend at the party. Even though I see her occasionally, I've never asked if she learned why her first husband's marriage ended in divorce. But they still seem happy together, and considering they've been married going on a dozen years now, I assume they've learned how to talk and solve any problems in their relationship—at least I hope they have. The key is to realize that you're moving toward a better relationship for both of you. As long as you're on the same page, things have a funny way of working themselves out.

⌒

ELISABETH'S STORY

I started dating a widower I met online. The first thing I noted and appreciated about Joe was his honesty. He dropped me a short line about our mutual interest in WWII history, and I checked out his profile. The very first line said, "I'm a widower and father of a nine-year-old girl." I thought that was courageous and refreshingly straightforward. Though I had told myself I would not date a single parent again, the fact that Joe was a widower made the situation different in my mind. As crass as it may seem, I felt there were advantages to dating a widower. For one thing, his marriage didn't end because it had failed, but for reasons beyond his control. For another, there weren't going to be annoying custody arguments and weekend-visitation issues that make so many other relationships practically impossible. There would also be no crazy ex-wife to put up with, or alimony arguments, or holiday tugs-of-war. I wrote him back.

After a couple of exchanges online, we moved to email and began an in-depth correspondence that went on for almost three weeks before we first met in person. Here again, Joe was very honest. I had a lot of questions for him, and while I pride myself at being tactful, some of my questions, while not technically difficult to answer, were not the sort that single men typically face. I've read a lot of stories from women who are frustrated because their widowers weren't honest about their feelings, their late wives, or about what they wanted for the future. Joe is not that kind of man, and, I suppose, I'm not the kind of woman who is afraid to ask direct (if tactful) questions.

I think that no matter the details of a past relationship, being open and honest with one's partner is crucial. Having a relationship with a widower offers very much the same challenges as any relationship—a man is a man, a woman is a woman, and people are people, when it comes down to it. Honesty and communication are crucial—period.

In the scores of emails exchanged before we met, Joe explained the basic details surrounding his late wife's death from cancer. He admitted that many of the women he'd dated since then had a difficult time with the subject, and that he had learned from each of those experiences and wanted to avoid making me uncomfortable. That's why he was quite forthcoming and even offered some information I didn't think to ask. He made it clear that while his wife's illness and death was by far the worst experience he'd ever gone through, he'd had a little over a year to prepare for the inevitable and do what he could to make plans to help his daughter through it. He wrote early on that by the time his wife passed away, he "was sad, but not devastated." As it turns out, his marriage had been deteriorating before his late wife was diagnosed, and while her remission offered hope of reparation, it didn't work. It may perhaps sound callous, but hearing that made me feel better.

Still, Joe waited over a year before he started dating again, because he was nervous about it and he wanted to be sure that he and his daughter were both ready. Here, again, he was honest, both with himself and with his daughter. He asked her how she'd feel about him having a girlfriend. (She gave him a thumbs-up.) He explained in another early email that he'd told her he was looking for someone who "would not be a replacement for Mom, but would be a good fit for us as a family."

He was also honest with me about the mistakes he had made after he started dating again. The more he shared, the more I was impressed with his straightforward approach to sharing his experiences, and the more I thought he would make an excellent partner.

I think you get the idea: At every stage of the relationship, Joe has been honest and open about what he's been through and where he'd like to go. I've tried to do the same for him, and it's been the most satisfying relationship I've ever had. The fact that he was once married to someone who is no longer living has had little, if any, bearing on our relationship. The fact that we are both open and honest with each other, however, has made all the difference.

CHAPTER 8

WHEN IT'S OVER, IT'S OVER: HOW TO AVOID GETTING BURNED AGAIN

UNFORTUNATELY, not every relationship with a widower is going to work out or even end well. There are lots of reasons relationships come to a close, but with a widower, it's usually because he isn't ready to move on, open his heart to someone else, or treat the new woman in his life like number one. But whether the relationship ends for those reasons or others, breaking up is still a distressing and difficult situation—especially if the relationship seemed promising at some point.

However, just because it ends doesn't mean it's over. Time and time again, I've seen the widower lure his recent breakup back into his web, only to burn her a second time. This chapter will help you walk away with your head held high and avoid being used and abused by widowers looking for someone to use and abuse.

HE SAYS HE'S CHANGED

The first thing that happens a few weeks after the relationship ends is that out of the blue the widower calls and tells you he wants to get back together. To entice you into his arms again, he'll say that he's had time to think things over and is going to change his behavior, and that he is finally ready to open his heart to you.

His offer can be very tempting—especially if you still have feelings for him. But I suggest that you don't readily agree to it. Widowers usually reach out to contact a past flame when they want one or more of the following three things:

- They're lonely and need someone to fill the void.

- They're horny and want nothing more than an outlet for their sexual desires.

- They miss having someone to wait on them hand and foot and need someone to take the place of the late wife.

Don't be fooled into thinking that the widower has suddenly come to his senses and wants to make you the center of his universe. There's no easier target for a manipulative widower than an ex-girlfriend—especially when he can play to her fantasy and claim he has miraculously overcome his grief and is ready to start afresh.

Widowers don't change their stripes unless they have a really good reason for doing so. If he treated you like a mistress, was stuck in perpetual grief, or made you feel like number two again and again, odds are, you're in for more or less the same kind of treatment the second time around. So if a widower contacts you after a breakup, save yourself further heartache and don't answer the phone or reply to his texts or emails. Your silence will speak louder than any returned phone call or text message you could send telling him it's over. Eventually he'll get the message and move on to someone else who hasn't wised up to the game he's playing.

If you think your widower's the exception to all of the above, and you want to reply to his overtures, I implore you to think long and hard before doing so and read Chapter 10: Giving Widowers a Second Chance.

I'm a big fan of the saying, "Fool me once, shame on you. Fool me twice, shame on me." If you end up getting burned a second time, you have no one to blame but yourself.

WANTING CLOSURE

The second way a woman gets burned again is when a relationship with a widower comes to a sudden, unexpected end, and she wants to know why. She reaches out to him to figure out what happened. When she doesn't get a satisfying answer from the widower, she thinks he hasn't told her the real reason. She keeps trying to get an answer and obsesses about it until she drives herself crazy.

Don't torture yourself like this. In the end, it doesn't matter if the relationship ended because there was another woman, if he was still in love with the late wife, or if he simply wasn't ready to move on. The widower isn't consumed by any of these thoughts. He's moved on to the next chapter of his life, and he isn't giving you a second thought. By focusing on the breakup and letting it occupy your thoughts, you're getting burned again and again and again.

When I ended things with Jennifer, the woman I seriously dated before Julianna, I just told her that things weren't working out, and that I was going to date someone else. It wasn't the best or classiest way to end things, but I just wanted the relationship to be over. I didn't spend a lot of time wondering if things could have worked out differently or how Jennifer was doing. Instead, I focused on Julianna and her wants and needs and moved on with my life. That's just the way guys think.

Jennifer, however, was in fits about it. Through a mutual friend, I heard that for a long time after the breakup, she kept expecting me to change my mind and come crawling back to her—something that was never, ever going to happen. Fortunately, Jennifer was eventually able to move on and find the love of her life, but she spent a lot of time wondering about things that made no difference in the end. Don't be like Jennifer. Focus on putting the pieces of your life back together and on being happy.

There's nothing wrong with having a good cry and a couple of "you" days to get him out of your system— that is natural and normal—but don't spend weeks or months brooding about what could have been done differently, or think that things will change if the widower gets back in touch. I guarantee you, the widower isn't worried about you. Instead, he's watching football, drinking a beer, and thinking about the next woman he can bring into his web. The quicker you can move on, the less power the widower—and the past—will have over you, and the sooner you can start a new and better chapter in your life.

SOPHIA'S STORY

A neighbor up the street became a widower after his wife and young daughter were killed by a drunk driver. We had only been neighborly up to that point, but my heart broke when I saw that he was left alone to raise a young son by himself. I took it upon myself to fix him homemade meals a couple of times a month. We became friends, and even though I wasn't looking for relationships, feelings for each other grew, and we started spending every free moment together.

At first things were good. He was attentive and did

things to make me feel special. I told him I wanted to take things slow, because his wife had only been gone a few short months. He respected my wishes. But after we got comfortable with each other, things started to change. We saw each other less, because he said he had to work late or that his son needed some one-on-one time with his dad.

Then, on the few times that we could get together, I noticed that the house hadn't changed one bit since his wife died. Her photos were everywhere, and her clothes were still in the closet. He wouldn't make even small changes for me, or agree to spend time at my house, where I would feel more comfortable.

Finally I couldn't take any more and had to end things. It was hard, and I cried myself to sleep every night for two weeks afterwards, even though I knew it was the right thing to do. Then, about a month after things ended, the widower called. Still feeling broken-hearted, I decided not to answer the phone. A few minutes later, there was a knock on my door. The widower stood outside with a bouquet of roses, saying that things would be different if I would only give him another chance. I wanted him to be telling the truth, that things had changed. I accepted the flowers and his apology, and we started seeing each other again.

It didn't take long to realize that nothing had changed. Her stuff was still everywhere, and he still found excuses not to spend time together or to come over to my place occasionally. I ended things a second time, but with considerably less heartache than the first time around.

Time passed, and I started dating someone who made me feel like the only person he had ever loved. A year later, we were engaged. During that time, the widower tried several times to get me to come back to him. Sometimes he used flowers. Other times he bought gifts he knew I'd like. Every time, I turned him down and said that my heart had been given to someone else.

In a couple months, I'll marry the man of my dreams. Even though things didn't work out with the widower, the experience taught me that men will treat you right if they really love and care about you. It made me appreciate my soon-to-be husband even more. I was willing to give my heart and soul to the widower, but he would not take it both times it was offered. Instead, I'll be living the rest of my life with someone else.

CHAPTER 9

FORGIVING A WIDOWER

WIDOWERS AREN'T PERFECT. Like anyone else, a widower will do and say things that are stupid, rude, and inconsiderate. Sometimes his words or actions can leave you feeling sad, angry, and frustrated. Other times, widowers end a relationship without any explanation, despite the fact that you've given your heart and soul to him. Whatever the situation, no matter the offense, it's vital that you forgive the widower for anything he's done to you.

Over the years, I've received emails from women who have suffered emotional, physical, financial, or other problems after widowers took advantage of them. Though these incidents left a lot of hurt feelings in their wake, and gave these women justification for the way they were feeling, I've always advised women to put the past behind them and move on. I've given the same advice to others who are just as upset over something small and unintentional a widower did, like calling his girlfriend by his late wife's name or forgetting an important anniversary.

Forgiveness is the process of letting go of the past and the pain you've experienced at the hands of others. As a result, you will find peace and regain control of your life. Instead of being angry, bitter, or upset about something the widower did, will you feel calm. Forgiving someone else is one of the greatest things we can do for ourselves. If you hold grudges and ill feelings toward others, you will never be able to be truly happy.

Depending on what the widower did, the hurt might always remain a part of your life, but forgiveness can lessen its grip and help you focus on other, more positive things. Forgiving someone doesn't mean that you deny the other person's responsibility for their actions or minimize or justify the wrong. It also doesn't mean that you become a doormat for the offender and let him continue to use and abuse you. Forgiving him means that if you think about him or happen to run into him when you're out and about, you're no longer filled with rage, resentment, or feelings of hostility.

In a perfect world, the widower who hurt you would acknowledge his mistakes and ask for your forgiveness. But our world is far from perfect, and we often find ourselves being harmed by someone who may not think they've done anything wrong, or who doesn't care if they've hurt you. That means you have to be able to forgive that person and let go of the pain.

MY JOURNEY OF FORGIVENESS

The importance of forgiveness is a lesson I learned personally while dating Julianna. As we were laying the foundation of our relationship, my heart and mind were still full of anger toward Krista for taking her own life, and, in the process, killing our unborn daughter. It didn't take long to realize that my fury toward her was stopping me from giving my heart to Julianna.

I was faced with a choice: I could continue feeling angry and resentful toward Krista, or I could forgive her and move on with my life. As I thought about what to do, I realized just how special Julianna was to me and that I would do anything to give our relationship a chance to turn into something that could last for the rest of our lives.

I wasn't sure how to go about forgiving Krista. She wasn't around to give me an apology or make amends for her actions. Still, I had to figure out a way to do it. I relied a lot on prayer and meditation. When anger welled up inside me, I worked on ways to dissipate the bad feelings and replace them with good ones. Instead of thinking about Krista, I'd shift my thoughts to Julianna or something else that made me happy. If that didn't work, I'd find something to keep my mind occupied, like reading a book or going to my grandmother's house to see if she needed help with something. Other times I'd throw myself into a project at work or at home, where I could concentrate on creating something that was beautiful and worthwhile. After a while, it became second nature to focus on positive and happy things instead of negative thoughts and feelings. It wasn't an easy process that happened overnight. There were days when I thought the anger and sadness would never go away. But piece by piece, I chipped away at the heart-ache and anguish that weighed on my soul.

Then one fall morning, all the anger and sadness simply disappeared.

It was a Saturday morning in early October. After waking up, I went to the kitchen to find something to eat. I happened to look outside the kitchen widow and caught a glimpse of the red, yellow, and orange leaves of the trees. I paused for a moment to take in the beautiful scene. As I looked at the leaves, my mind drifted to Krista. For the first time since she'd killed herself, I was able to think about her without feeling angry or sad. Instead, I was filled with a strong feeling of peace. In that moment, the burden that had been weighing me down disappeared. I started crying, because it felt so good to be free of the hatred and animosity that had been holding me back. I knew that I could finally start a new chapter in my life with Julianna.

Things moved forward, and we were married soon after this incident. Since we've tied the knot, we've both had to forgive each other for stupid things we've said and done. (Though, to be honest, I think she's had to forgive me many times more than I've had to forgive her.) Because we've done a good job of not holding grudges over big or little mistakes, we've been able to have a strong and successful marriage.

5 SUGGESTIONS TO GET STARTED

Forgiveness isn't a one-size-fits-all solution. How to go about forgiving someone differs from one person to another. My journey involved a lot of prayer, contemplation, and reflection. That may or may not work for you. Whatever it is that you need to forgive, here are five suggestions that can help you get started on your journey toward peace and happiness.

1. **Get rid of anything that reminds you of the pain.** There's something cathartic about getting rid of objects that remind you of a bad experience. If you have pictures, jewelry, knickknacks, or anything else that brings back resentment and anguish, throw them away. If there are photos, emails, or other forms of electronic communication on your computer, delete them. Block the widower from your phone, email address, and social media accounts so he can't reach out and hurt you again.

Anything that stokes the fires of anger and resentment will only hold you back. It's better to get rid of anything that reminds you of him and your experiences with him so you can focus on healing yourself and moving on.

2. **Have one good venting session.** Whether it's talking to a friend, going someplace private to scream at the top of their lungs, or writing their feelings out on paper, most people need a physical way of releasing all their anger and other negative feelings. Make it a good one, because, in order for it to be truly effective, you need to get it all out at once. Doing it over and over again won't help. If anything, venting a second or third time makes things worse.

3. **Don't seek revenge.** When someone hurts us, it's normal to want to get even to let them feel the pain we're experiencing. But revenge is like cancer; it slowly spreads until it consumes your entire body. It crowds out positive goal setting and other constructive things you can be doing that will help you be happy again. In the long run, seeking revenge

makes a bad situation worse. Even if it initially brings you pleasure, it's something you'll eventually regret. Hold your head up and don't lower yourself to the level of the person who hurt you. Instead, focus on making your life one that can bless the lives of those around you.

4. **Stop thinking like a victim**. You have no control over the decisions or thoughts of others. What happened, happened. Stop seeing yourself as a victim of another's actions. Widowers fall into this trap all the time by identifying themselves as someone who's lost a spouse. If you've dated a man who doesn't want to shed the widower label, you've seen firsthand how absolutely destructive that can be. All they focus on is their loss and their grief. They think they're entitled to other's pity and compassion. As a result, they're never able to move on and be happy again. If you want to let an unfortunate event define your life and control your future, fine. But people will grow tired of it, and you'll find yourself all alone in the end. Don't let someone's hurtful words or actions define or limit

your future. When you take your life back, you'll discover that the power the offending person had in your life has vanished.

5. **Do something good for someone else.** There's always someone out there who is hurting more than you. Try to do at least one kind thing for someone every day. It can be a co-worker, family member, friend, neighbor, or a complete stranger. Doing good for others, and turning your thoughts to those who are suffering, will help you find that inner peace you seek. The times I reached out to help or comfort others, even though I was still hurting, are the moments when I took the biggest steps toward forgiving Krista.

When a widower says or does something stupid, insensitive, or cruel, you have to be willing to stand up, dust yourself off, and forgive him. It doesn't matter if the widower's infraction was big or small. Don't let anger, hatred, or other ill feelings canker your soul. I don't know where my life would be had I let bitterness and resentment take it over, but I know I wouldn't be married to Julianna or have the family and happiness I enjoy today. Forgive, forget, and move on with life. It may not be the easiest thing you've ever done, but it will be the greatest choice you can make toward living a happy and fulfilling life.

~

MARTHA'S STORY

My widower and I had been seeing each other for six months when our first Thanksgiving came along. That morning he emailed me and said, "Happy Thanksgiving!" then went to spend the day with his family. I was excluded because his parents didn't know about me, although he had told me he loved me the month before. My parents are both deceased, so I had no plans for the day and ended up staying home alone.

Of all the widower issues I've dealt with, being kept a secret for so long was one of the most hurtful. I believe he kept the secret because he was worried what people would think, since his late wife had only been gone for nine months when we started seeing each other. Even so, it made me feel less than special.

When he called late that night, I told him how hurt

I was to have been excluded from his family gathering. As a result, he began to introduce me to his friends and coworkers. As I saw the change, I was truly able to forgive him and get over the disappointment I'd felt earlier. We even enjoyed a very nice Christmas get-together with his family! After he recognized the feelings of rejection he had caused me, he made sure to introduce me to everyone important to him. I've been included in every family gathering since that first Christmas. He even invited me to a special dinner held in his honor for seventeen years of service with his company.

He and his daughter are still close with his late wife's brother and his family, who live out of state. When they came into town for a visit, he made a special point of having us meet so we could get acquainted. And last but not least, I attended his cousin's huge wedding, where I met relatives he hadn't seen in years.

Had he expected me to remain a secret girlfriend, I doubt very seriously that this relationship would have worked. Based on the fact that he was receptive to my feelings and willing to make the necessary changes, we were able to move forward.

That particular Thanksgiving was a little over two years ago. We're now engaged, and he wastes no time introducing me to everyone. I believe that open communication about our feelings is a key factor in having a good relationship with a widower.

CHAPTER 10

GIVING WIDOWERS A SECOND CHANCE

RELATIONSHIPS WITH WIDOWERS can end for any number of reasons. Some widowers simply aren't ready to open their hearts to someone else. Other times, the widower is still getting his dating legs and simply isn't ready for a committed relationship. Whatever the reason for the breakup, it's common for widowers to reach out weeks or months later, apologize for their behavior, and ask for a second chance.

Getting back together with a widower is risky, because it's hard to tell how serious he is about starting anew. Anyone can *say* they've changed, but actually changing one's thoughts, actions, and habits is extremely difficult unless that person has a powerful reason to modify their behavior. For example, people with drug or alcohol addictions generally aren't motivated to kick the habit and get sober until they've hit rock bottom. Widowers have little or no motivation to open their heart and start a new life with someone else unless they really and truly find someone they can spend the rest of their lives with.

Most widowers who want a second chance miss the companionship, sex, and other benefits that come with a relationship, and they see you as an easy target. Sometimes things change for a short period, but most widowers won't be able to follow through with their promises unless they value and love you as much as they did the late wife. It doesn't take long for most women who get back together with a widower to realize they've been duped.

WHEN DO WIDOWERS DESERVE A SECOND CHANCE?

Because each situation is unique, it's impossible to say whether or not you should give your widower another shot. But here are some general guidelines to help you think through your situation and make the best possible decision based on your knowledge and circumstances.

- **Don't make the decision on a whim.** Often, relationship decisions are based on emotion instead of thought and deliberation. It's easy to give a widower a second chance if you still have strong feelings for him or think the relationship is filled with potential. If he wants another crack at things, don't give him an answer right then. Instead, spend some time alone, thinking long and hard about whether he deserves it and is ready to move forward with you. Weigh the pros and cons of opening your heart again to someone who's already hurt you once. If you have doubts, don't be afraid to follow your gut and say no. You'll be glad you did.

- **What would you do if he weren't a widower?** Take the fact that he's a widower out of the equation. Would you give a single or divorced man the same second chance if the relationship had ended in a similar fashion? If not, then why are you letting the widower's marital status change the way you approach the situation? Don't go soft or make excuses just because he's a widower. He's a man first and foremost. He will act and behave like a man. The fact that he lost his wife changes nothing. Don't give a widower a second chance that you wouldn't give someone else.

- **Don't return to an abuser.** If he has been mentally, physically, or verbally abusive to you, **DO NOT** bring him back in your life under any circumstances. Abusive behavior isn't something that can be changed overnight. Allowing yourself back into a hurtful situation is placing your mental, physical, and emotional health at risk. It's not worth putting yourself in danger again just because someone says they've changed. There are no second chances for those who are abusive. They've had their chance and lost it forever. Never, ever, get back in the clutches of someone who doesn't show the proper respect.

- **Draw a line in the sand.** Decide what behavior you won't tolerate the second time around. Let him know where that line is, and, if he crosses it, the relationship is over. Widowers who are sincere about putting you first will not only agree to the terms you lay down, they won't even attempt to violate them. If he tests you by crossing the line, it's vital that you follow through and end things immediately. Widowers will take advantage of any sign of weakness you display or excuses you make for him. If you don't end things, he'll continue to redraw your line for you instead of showing you the love and respect you deserve.

- **Actions speak louder than words.** Men say what they mean through their actions—not their words. If the widower promises to make changes, have him follow through on his words with his actions *before* you get back together with him. For example, if he promises to take down the photos of his late wife, have him follow through on that before you agree to get back together. If he drags his feet or comes up with excuses for why he hasn't done it yet, odds are, he's looking to use you as an emotional crutch and isn't serious about treating you like a queen.

I write this chapter as someone who *wouldn't* be married to Julianna if it weren't for the second chance she gave me. Those who have read *Room for Two* know that our first date was a complete and utter disaster. If Julianna hadn't heeded her father's suggestion and given me another chance, we wouldn't be married, and this book might have never been written.

My second chance only worked out because I loved Julianna from the first moment I saw her, and I was willing to do what it took. When I got my second chance, I wanted a serious relationship with her more than anything. I valued her feelings and needs more than my grief or any love I had for my late wife. I moved forward because I wanted to make Julianna the center of my universe. I needed a strong reason to take that step, and there wasn't a better reason than her.

So should you give your widower a second chance? Only you can answer that question. Generally, I advise against it. Most women who have given their widower second, third, or even fourth chances generally end up getting their heart broken time and time again. However, if your gut (not your heart) tells you he's worthy of a second chance, let him know in no uncertain terms what needs to change, how you expect to be treated, and that if you have the feeling he's not ready to move on, you won't hesitate to end things. Remember, the saying "Fool me once, shame on you. Fool me twice, shame on me" applies here. If you ignore the red flags and doubts the second time around, you've got no one to blame but yourself.

∽

KATE'S STORY

I met my twenty-seven-year-old widower two months after his wife passed away from a terminal illness. He specifically stated that he didn't want to date but just was looking for a friend. I seemed like a natural option, since I already knew his late wife's family and didn't need any explanations about his situation. At the same time, I was not close enough to be a painful reminder of his past.

After a few weeks of conversations over email and dinners, we both acknowledged that we felt more than platonic friendship. Sensing that a widower would bring unique issues to dating, I suggested we let things progress according to his comfort level. He assured me he'd worked through his grief and felt ready to move forward with me. From there, we promised to be direct and honest about our feelings, openly discussing serious topics like his late wife and what we sought in a relationship. We even received the gracious support of his late wife's parents, who were comforted to see him happy again.

Taking into consideration his young daughter and my moral beliefs, we developed our relationship slowly on a physical level but moved forward more quickly on an emotional level. Prayer and reflection instilled a sense of peace in me when contemplating a potential future with someone who would always hold a special place in his heart for another woman. His character and his caring behavior toward me (even strongly defending his decision to pursue our relationship to concerned family and friends) made our relationship seem worth the inevitable complications. When he voluntarily shared that he could see a future together, he seemed to confirm that we both stood on the same page.

Then over Christmas, he confronted a surge of conflicting emotions and questioned whether he truly was ready for a relationship. He decided we should just be friends, explaining he'd rather have me in his life that way than not at all. But I had already begun to fall in love. I couldn't conceptualize how to be "just a friend." Still, I rationalized that maybe over time, friendship would lead back to a relationship, although there was no guarantee.

I couldn't deny my feelings for him or make him want to date me, but I couldn't be *that* girl who follows a guy around, desperately hoping he'll eventually pick her. I also considered that if I couldn't be a stable presence in his daughter's life, it would be unfair to set her up for future heartache too.

I understood that he needed to face this complicated wave of grief on his own. In order to make his life a little less complicated, I told him I would step back to give him space to deal with his issues without our friendship being a confusing factor on the sidelines. I still believed in the potential we could have as a couple down the road, but realized it would only work if he felt completely at peace in a relationship with me. Ultimately, I drew courage to end the relationship from the words Saint Paul wrote in 1 Corinthians 13:4-5:

"Love is always patient and kind ... and never seeks its own advantage." If I truly loved him, I needed to put my happiness aside and be patient while he grieved. And if he came back to me, I could confidently know he was ready to be together for the right reasons.

It's been almost a year since I last saw or talked to my widower. Since our breakup, he has chosen to become serious with someone else. My choice to walk away was the hardest decision I've ever made, and honestly, it's been a long and painful process to fully let go. I am content, however, knowing my decision came from love, from placing the needs of two other people ahead of my selfish desire for what would have resulted in only an illusion of a fulfilling relationship.

I can look at myself in the mirror, proud that I trusted my instincts and did not sacrifice my values. And fortunately, with the pain came many blessings: An even closer relationship with my parents, a special friendship with the widower's in-laws, and hope that God has planned even greater love for me, in time.

CHAPTER 11

10 THINGS YOU CAN LEARN FROM OTHER WIDOWER RELATIONSHIPS

As I WAS WRITING THIS BOOK, the thought hit me that I've been giving advice on widower relationships for over a decade. I can still clearly remember the first email I received with a widower question. I remember being puzzled and wondering why on earth someone would actually reach out to an anonymous blogger who was still trying to get his dating legs back. I answered the question to the best of my ability and went on with life. A week later, another email arrived. Four days later, I got a third one. By the time I married Julianna, the email trickle had turned into a flood. And in the ensuing years, it hasn't let up.

Even though the circumstances of those who email me have all been different, I've noticed some patterns and themes repeating themselves. So in the final chapter of this book, I'm going to share the collective wisdom from the thousands of stories and experiences that have entered my inbox. If nothing else, I hope it can help you avoid the mistakes and pitfalls that others have encountered.

1. **Don't lower your standards.** It's never worth setting aside your own values when dating a widower. Doing so will *always* lead to regret and disappointment down the road. Lowering your standards or excusing a widower's bad behavior won't make him love you more or help him overcome his grief. Be yourself and hold the widower to the same expectations you have for any other guy. If he can't love and appreciate you for who you really are, you'll always be in an unfulfilling relationship.

2. **You can't do anything to help a widower overcome his grief or move on.** There are no words you can say or actions you can take that will help a

widower take down the photos of the late wife or make you feel like the center of his universe. Grief and love exist in one's heart and mind. Widowers choose to be happy or sad, move forward or wallow in their grief. The widower has to *want* to move on before he can fall in love again. It doesn't matter how many sacrifices you make for him or how much you love and care about him—a widower will only move on if he believes you're worth it. All you can do is be the wonderful, beautiful person you already are. If that's not enough for him, it's not because of anything you said or did. It just means that he doesn't love you enough to undertake the necessary changes and sacrifices to make you number one.

3. **If it's meant to be, it will work out.** I don't believe in fate or that there's only one person who can be our soul mate. Rather, I believe that through our own choices, we decide our destiny. But I also believe that if two people have that special connection, the relationship usually works out, despite mistakes made along the way. If both people want

something badly enough, things have a tendency to fall into place. It was that way in my relationship with my late wife and in my relationship with Julianna. I've seen friends and family members experience something similar in their relationships, and I've seen many widowers and their new loves experience it too. If it's meant to be, things just have a way of working out.

4. **Don't get serious quickly.** The widower might act like the perfect guy the first few weeks you know him, but that doesn't mean he's ready to put his past life and his old ways to the side. It takes a while for a widower to sort out his feelings and decide if what he feels is really love or just the desire to have someone in his life. Keep this in mind before you sleep with him or start making plans for a wedding. It can take two or three months for a widower to figure out how he really feels about you and to reveal his true character. If things are still looking good after that amount of time, then you can start thinking more long term.

5. **Don't waste your life**. It doesn't take years to know if the widower is ready to give you the number-one place in his heart. In fact, it generally takes a year or less. If you've been together for more than a year and you still feel like you're living in the shadow of the late wife, you're better off ending the relationship. Additional time isn't going to change things. He'll still feel the same way at two years, five years, and ten years. Life is too short to spend precious months and years with someone who's not ready to give his heart and soul to you.

6. **It doesn't matter what anyone else thinks**. It doesn't matter if the widower's children think he's moving on too fast. Nor does it matter if your kids think he's not right for you. It doesn't matter if his family thinks he's disrespecting his late wife's memory by starting a new relationship. In the end, everyone else's opinions are just distractions from what really matters: What you think of each other and whether you're willing to give the time, energy, and commitment necessary for your relationship to blossom and become something beautiful.

7. **The late wife won't be a constant presence in your relationship**. As time goes by, the late wife will play less of a role in your relationship. At first, it may seem that everyone is comparing you to the late wife and that she keeps popping up in conversations or at other inopportune times. As time goes on, and your relationship with the widower grows stronger, it will become more about the two of you and your future together and less about the late wife and the widower's past. And it will all happen faster than you think.

8. **Never settle**. Don't settle for a man you can't be happy with. The habits, attitudes, and behaviors he has now are the same ones he'll have five, ten, or twenty years down the road. If you have problems with any of his thoughts, words, or actions today, you're going to have the same problems when you're old and gray. Don't deceive yourself by thinking your relationship will get better once he has more time to think things over. They won't. Whether you've settled for someone who can't meet your expectations, or you're living in the

constant shadow of the late wife, you'll never be happy. If you want your husband to treat you like number one, find someone who is already everything you want him to be.

9. **Widowers who are ready to move on will move on.** Men who want you to be the most important person in their lives don't make excuses about why things aren't moving forward. They simply put one foot in front of the other. Grief and other late-wife issues will be put to the side once a widower has found the right person for him. They don't play mind games or suddenly decide that they need time to think things over. They move forward to make it happen.

10. **You're not on the same level as the late wife unless you're married.** There's a difference between being married and not being married. No matter what the widower says, you'll never be on the same level as the late wife until he puts a ring on your finger. I know that not everyone wants to get married, but don't deceive yourself into thinking it doesn't matter, because it does. When and how soon to get

married is up to you, but until you exchange vows, the late wife is always going to occupy a slightly higher spot in their heart. If the widower loves you as much as he loved the late wife, he should be willing to give you his hand in marriage just like he did with the late wife.

Take heed of this collective wisdom from others and use it to your best advantage as you navigate the waters of dating a widower. It can save you heartache and help you avoid unfortunate situations and circumstances. I wish you the very best in your relationship with a widower and hope you can move forward and have a successful, fulfilling relationship.

~

TAMMY'S STORY

As the divorced mom of two young boys, I decided to join an online dating service. One thing I was sure about was that I wasn't going to settle for just any man. My boys and I deserve more than that.

I came across the profile of a widower with three

children. I felt an immediate connection and sent him an email. We met for lunch the next day. The chemistry was immediate, and neither of us wanted lunch to end. We casually saw each other for four months. We talked about how he managed work, grief, children, and his life. It was all very admirable. However, my gut told me that he was not even close to moving on. His wife had only died two-and-a-half months prior. Yep, a huge red flag to me. But I had dated enough to know that the connection I felt was rare and decided to push those thoughts aside and pursue "us."

It turned out that his life was consumed with everything except me. We texted and talked regularly, but were only able to see each other for an hour here and there. I developed strong feelings for him, and he said the most incredible things to me, but after a couple of months, I realized he was not ready to move on and give me the respect I deserve and the relationship I want.

Often, we can understand something in our heads but feel differently in our hearts. I tried to break it off several times, but kept coming back to him. Finally I ended it for good, even though I still wanted to be there for him. I know that my boys and I deserve to be someone's number-one priority. I am not that for him right now and not sure if I ever can be. Do I wish I had followed my gut feeling when we first met and not pursued the relationship? A part of me does, but I also believe that people come into our lives when we need them to and for a reason. I feel that we were meant to meet. I have learned a lot about myself and have been there for him when he needed me. I feel good about that.

Eventually I had to move on and give myself the respect I deserve. I had to stop betraying myself and my desire to be in a loving, healthy, committed relationship with someone who is as ready as I am. The widower is an amazing person and dad, and I know we could be phenomenal together, but life isn't always clean and easy, and sometimes things don't work out. It's tough to admit and even tougher sometimes for the heart to realize that.

LINDA'S STORY

We began dating twenty-one months after his wife passed away from breast cancer. He assured me he was healed and ready for a relationship, and since I'm trust-ing, I believed him. He had been dating six months be-fore he met me, so I didn't feel I was a rebound. What I didn't realize then is that a widower doesn't truly know he's not ready until he's in that new relationship.

He had two daughters, ages five and seven, and we bonded immediately and intensely. I was crazy about him, and he said he felt the same. He mentioned mar-riage, and I let him know we needed to take our time to be sure he was completely healed. All was great for a couple of months, and then he started talking about his late wife quite a bit. Initially, it didn't bother me. However, as our relationship and my feelings grew, it began to nag at me. If I said I liked something, he re-plied that the late wife liked that, did that, wanted to do that—you get the drift.

After a couple of months, I let him know that con-tinually talking about her was creating insecurity in me about how he really felt and whether he was indeed ready. He said he did that because he was voicing his memories of her when they were triggered. I let him know that some things about his life with another woman should be kept to himself so as not to hurt me.

He apologized and said he understood. He cut way back on mentioning her, so I was comfortable when he did happen to make a comment here and there.

We talked about where he was emotionally, and during one of these talks, I asked him not to drag me and the girls down this road if he didn't feel he was ready to commit or if I wasn't the right person. He promised he would never do that to us—he loved us. We were intimate right away, and it was a closeness I had never experienced before. Once the foreplay began, he would sneeze, and he said the only other person he had that with was his late wife, and that was a very good sign about us.

That lasted right up until about a couple of weeks prior to me ending our eight-month relationship. We drove to his hometown, and I met one of his brothers. A few weeks later, he took me to his family reunion and introduced me as his girlfriend. We took a road trip together, including my two grandsons, and spent a week touring Route 66. We had a wonderful time, and I felt we were really moving forward.

It was late when we arrived back at his house. I was exhausted, so I lay on the couch and took a brief nap. I woke up and could tell something was bothering him, so I asked him what was wrong. He said he was upset that I was sleeping while he was watching his two girls, my two grandsons, and trying to put things away. I reminded him that I've taken care of his girls many, many times so he could nap and sleep in, and that was not fair. I had this nagging feeling that something else was bothering him.

We went outside, and I let him know that he needed to be honest with me about his feelings. After pacing for a few minutes, he said he didn't think he was ready to love me like he loved his late wife. He said he was happy, but just going through the motions, and he didn't know if he just wasn't ready or if things had moved too fast for him.

My heart dropped into my feet. I was floored, devastated. I felt betrayed and misled—I was angry. I told him I would make it easy for him, gave him a hug, went inside, and told the girls goodbye. I hugged the five-year-old and told her I would always love her and to be good for Daddy. I hugged the seven-year-old, told her the same thing, and as hard as I tried, I just couldn't hold back my tears. I broke down. She sat up and asked what was wrong, and I told her I had to go.

I'd fallen in love with my widower, but the voice inside me prevented me from falling completely. He emailed me a few days later, saying he wanted to be friends. I agreed, and a month later, asked if the girls could spend the day with me. I picked them up, and he was eager to talk, sat next to me, showed me the girls' report cards like he always did, smiled a lot, acted nervous, and asked me how I had been. I smiled and answered his questions, but was hurting inside. I let him know we needed to go because, we had things to do. That was true, but I really just needed to get out of there. Seeing him was a painful reminder of what we would never have.

The girls and I had a fantastic day. I love them to pieces, but when I dropped them off that evening, I knew it would be the last time I saw them. Reality set in that day. He would someday find a new love, and because the girls are so young, they would need to bond with the new woman, so my being in the picture would make that more difficult. I lost more than his love—I lost their love too, and it's heartbreaking.

∽

KAREN'S STORY

I never would have married my husband had I not been at peace with his past. Yet even though I was comfortable talking about his late wife and was fond of her family, I would hardly say that I felt close to this woman who'd died four years before I came onto the scene. All that changed after I was diagnosed with uterine cancer.

Thankfully, my surgery went smoothly, the tumor was caught early, and my prognosis is excellent.

Still, cancer has been the most difficult experience of my life to date. For months, I lived in a cocoon of fear, anxiety, and vulnerability.

My husband was a rock, being my best friend and confidant throughout every moment. But I wanted to know how other cancer survivors dealt with the emotional side effects.

I'm not sure why, but I turned to my husband's late wife. Over a seventeen-year period, she survived three rounds of colon cancer and two bouts of leukemia, but not the third.

How did she wait out those long days before the test results came back? How did she manage the pain of radiation, the nausea of chemo? Did she cry? Who did she talk to about her fears? Did friends treat her differently? Did she get angry when doctors gave her evasive answers? Of course, it was up to my husband to act as an intermediary. I asked the questions, and he calmly, honestly answered them, never editorializing or eulogizing.

Learning how she navigated the emotions of her illnesses made me feel less lonely, less crazy. I always admired her, but now I feel that if we had known each other in real life, we could have been friends.

The experience has also made me feel even closer to my husband, whose allegiance is never in doubt when we bring his late wife into a conversation. He honors and cherishes his past, but he lives and loves in the now.

This would be a nice place to end the story of my first year of being happily married to a widower, but there is another unexpected postscript. Six months after my surgery, my husband had a mild heart attack that scared the crap out of both of us. And it made me realize how devastated I would be to lose him so soon.

Luckily, with a new stent and medication, and a commitment to eating better and exercising more, chances are good that he will be around for a while. Me, too.

And that's pretty cool because in sickness *and* in health, we really have a good thing going.

ABOUT THE AUTHOR

 AT THE AGE OF 26, Abel Keogh unexpectedly found himself a young widower. When he decided to start dating again he looked in vain for resources that could guide him through the dating waters and open his heart to someone else. He found nothing. As he began blogging about his experiences, women dating widowers began emailing him asking for his thoughts on their situations. As the numbers of emails increased, Abel started writing a weekly dating a widower advice column called *Widower Wednesday* as well as the books *Dating a Widower: Starting a Relationship with a Man Who's Staring Over* and *Marrying a Widower: What you Need to Know before Tying the Knot.*

Abel is also the author of the memoir *Room for Two*—the story of the year of his life following his late wife's suicide—and the novel *The Third.* He and his wife Julianna are the parents of three boys and two girls. Learn more at www.abelkeogh.com.

ACKNOWLEDGMENTS

FIRST I'D LIKE TO THANK all the women who submitted stories to this book. It takes courage to share their stories and I appreciate your willingness to share them with the world.

In addition I'd like to thank Fran Platt for her awesome cover design and typesetting, Tristi Pinkston, Lu Ann Staheli, Annette Lyon, and Melody Haras for their editing and proofreading suggestions.

Most of all, I'd like to thank Julianna for giving me the time to write a yet another book that opened up parts of our lives for others to learn from. None of my books are possible without your love and support. Having you in my life is the best thing that ever happened to me.

Made in the USA
Columbia, SC
14 April 2024

34370151R00075